BUGS FOR DINNER?

The Eating Habits of Neighborhood Creatures

By Sam and Beryl Epstein

Illustrated by Walter Gaffney-Kessell

Macmillan Publishing Company
New York

To Roger Beaudry
—W. G.-K.

Text copyright © 1989 by Sam Epstein and Beryl Epstein
Illustrations copyright © 1989 by Walter Gaffney-Kessell
All rights reserved. No part of this book may be reproduced
or transmitted in any form or by any means, electronic or
mechanical, including photocopying, recording, or by any
information storage and retrieval system, without
permission in writing from the Publisher.
Macmillan Publishing Company
866 Third Avenue, New York, NY 10022
Collier Macmillan Canada, Inc.
First Edition
Printed in the United States of America

10   9   8   7   6   5   4   3   2   1

The text of this book is set in 12 point Berkeley Old Style Book.
The illustrations are rendered in pen-and-ink.

Library of Congress Cataloging-in-Publication Data
Epstein, Sam, date.
Bugs for dinner? : the eating habits of
neighborhood creatures / by Sam and Beryl Epstein ;
illustrated by Walter Gaffney-Kessell. — 1st ed.   p.   cm.
Summary: Recounts how squirrels, robins, grasshoppers,
and other creatures in an urban environment find
their food and avoid being eaten themselves.
ISBN 0-02-733501-1
1. Animals—Food—Juvenile literature. 2. Urban fauna—
Food—Juvenile literature. [1. Urban animals—Food.
2. Animals—Food.] I. Epstein, Beryl Williams, date.
II. Gaffney-Kessell, Walter, ill. III. Title.
QL756.5.E67   1989   591.53—dc19   88-26654   CIP   AC

·Contents·

Could you live on the weeds growing in a vacant lot? Or on the flowers and insects in a yard? Or on the leaves and seeds in a city park? Most people couldn't. But the many creatures that live in those places find all their food there.

Some of them—squirrels and birds, for example—have to provide food for their babies, as well as for themselves. Some have an even bigger task. Every bee you see is a food-seeker for the thousands of bees inside its beehive. Every ant you see is seeking food for the ants that never leave their ant nest. And all of these tireless food-seekers are in danger of being eaten by some creature larger or stronger or more clever than they are!

·SQUIRRELS·

The soft fluffy fur of squirrels may be gray or black or a reddish brown. Their bodies, about eight inches long, have bushy tails of about the same length. Each squirrel weighs around one pound and needs two pounds of food a week. So squirrels eat almost anything they can find.

In the spring they eat leaf buds, tender new bark, and the sweet sap that comes from some trees. They rob birds' nests of their eggs, and eat baby birds, too, if they get the chance.

In the summer they feast on wild cherries and grapes, and on apples, peaches, and other fruits. They eat insects and mushrooms, as well.

In the autumn they eat nuts and all kinds of seeds. They also store away some of these foods to live on during the coming winter, when all food will be scarce.

To store an acorn, for example, a squirrel first claws a hole in the ground, an inch or more deep. Then it pushes in the acorn, fills the hole with dirt patted snugly down, and covers the spot with leaves and twigs.

When the weather turns cold and food becomes scarce, a squirrel's sharp sense of smell helps it find buried food. But if you see a squirrel dig up an acorn, you can't be sure that that acorn was buried by that squirrel. Probably the squirrel itself can't be sure.

Squirrels can climb trees and vines to reach high-growing fruits and berries. They can run out to the very end of a slender tree branch, and hang there by their hind feet so their front claws can reach a pear dangling from the tip of the branch.

They can push off an acorn's cap and chew off its shell to get at the kernel inside. They can gnaw through the harder shells of hickory nuts, butternuts, and walnuts, and then poke out the nutmeat with their sharp teeth.

A squirrel can even steal food from a bird feeder people put in a place they were sure only birds could reach. Can you guess how a squirrel might steal seed from a feeder hanging from a long wire fastened to a porch roof?

This is one way: The squirrel climbs a tree near the porch and leaps from the end of a branch to the porch roof. Then the squirrel takes the wire between its front paws and swings the feeder back and forth, faster and faster. When the seeds inside the feeder fly out and fall, the squirrel leaps back to the branch, runs down the tree trunk, and eats its fill of the seeds now scattered on the ground.

Squirrels are very messy eaters. If you see a litter of seed husks and stems beneath a maple tree, you can be sure a squirrel spit them out as it sat on the branch above, chewing up the seed clusters it found there.

If you see husks and a chewed-up pinecone on a stump or a flat stone, you'll know a squirrel recently ate a meal there. Sitting up straight, balanced by its tail, the squirrel held the pinecone in its front claws as you might hold an ear of corn in your hands. It turned the pinecone as it ate and moved the cone back and forth, chewing off one row of seeds after another. As the squirrel ate, it spit out the seed husks, and when it was finished it dropped the cone on top of them.

In the spring, when food is plentiful, baby squirrels are born. But like human babies, they cannot feed themselves. A mother squirrel nurses its tiny naked babies for several weeks. During that time they stay in the ball-shaped nest, made of twigs and leaves, which the mother has built high in a tree. There they are usually safe from climbing and flying creatures such as snakes, raccoons, and owls, which would like to eat them.

Once their fur is grown and the baby squirrels leave the nest to find their own food, they are in danger chiefly from the cats and dogs that try to catch and eat any squirrel they see. But squirrels can almost always outclimb or outrun these animals. So their most dangerous enemies are human beings, whose cars run over them or who hunt them for sport—or because they like to eat squirrel meat themselves.

·SPARROWS, ROBINS, AND PIGEONS·

Sparrows, robins, and pigeons are three very different birds, but they are alike in one way: They're not afraid of living near human beings. So you're likely to notice these birds in yards, parks, and vacant lots.

You might see a sparrow or a robin fly to its nest in a tree or bush right beside your door. You might see a pigeon nesting on the windowsill of an apartment house. And they might all come near you if you sat on the grass eating your lunch. They would be waiting to pick up crumbs you dropped—or the birdseed you might have brought along just for them. The sparrows and pigeons might come so close that you would think they wanted to eat out of your hand.

All sparrows are small. One of the most common, called the *chipping sparrow*, measures only about five inches from the tip of its black bill to the tip of its tail. It has a chestnut-colored patch, like a small cap, on the top of its head. The cap has a white border on each side. Below that border is a thin black line that seems to run straight through the sparrow's eye. Its breast is a soft gray, and its back and tail feathers are brown and white.

As it hops busily about, the chipping sparrow picks up the grass seeds and weed seeds that form most of its diet. Sometimes it eats insects, too.

Sparrows, like all birds, have no teeth and can't chew their food before swallowing it. So this is what happens to a sparrow's food—and the food of other birds—when it is swallowed: The

food, along with small stones the bird picked up as it ate, goes down the sparrow's throat into a storage pouch called a *crop*. There the food is partly digested.

Next, with the small stones, the partly digested food goes down into an extra stomach called a *gizzard*. Strong muscles in the walls of the gizzard squeeze everything together and grind the stones against the food. When the food becomes soft, it finally passes into the real stomach, where it is completely digested. If the bird has swallowed tiny bits of feather or bone or anything else it can't digest, it coughs them up and casts them out.

Like most birds, sparrows feed their nesting baby birds by *regurgitating*. That is, they bring up into their mouths some of the partly digested food in their crops. Then, with their beaks, they poke that food into the wide-open mouths of their babies.

Robins are red-breasted, grayish brown birds almost twice as large as chipping sparrows. They measure about ten inches from

crop

stomach

gizzard

the tips of their beaks to the tips of their tails. They sometimes eat berries and fruits, but they live chiefly on earthworms, spiders, and insects such as grasshoppers, beetles, caterpillars, termites, and butterflies.

A robin doesn't always hop along the ground looking for food, as most birds do. It often runs, and it can run pretty fast. When a robin sees something to eat, it stops suddenly and tilts its head to one side. This lets the eye on that side of its head get a good look at what the robin has found. Then its beak darts swiftly downward and snatches up a mouthful of food.

Sometimes a robin grabs the head of a worm sticking out of a hole and tugs at it, and the worm's head breaks off. The startled robin may lose its balance and almost topple over backward, but it usually manages to keep hold of the piece of worm in its beak.

Pigeons also measure about ten inches from the tips of their beaks to the tips of their tails, but, unlike robins, they are not all the same color. A pigeon may be white, pale tan, silvery, or dark gray. It may have markings of black or white or brown or some brighter color.

Pigeons eat berries, fruits, and seeds. They feed their babies as other birds do, by bringing food up from their crops. But some of the food in their crops changes into a white liquid, so baby pigeons are given what is called *pigeon milk*.

Sparrows, robins, and pigeons have many enemies that would like to eat them. Among these are squirrels, which rob the birds' nests of eggs and baby birds. Dogs and cats chase the birds when they are on the ground. Hawks swoop down on them, their talons stretched out to snatch up a meal. Hawks also chase birds in the air, and catch them if they can't find a safe hiding place.

Birds see and hear very well, so they can keep a sharp watch for their enemies. But a bird's ability to store food in its crop is probably its best protection. When it finds a good source of food, a bird quickly gobbles it up and lets the food collect in its crop. Then it flies off to a safe perch and rests there, while the food it has eaten passes through its gizzard and is digested.

·HONEYBEES·

Every honeybee you see on a flower is a worker bee busy at its job of gathering food. This tiny black and yellow insect, about half an inch long, has two pairs of wings and six legs. Its body is perfectly designed to collect the two substances bees live on and carry them home to its hive. Both of these substances are found inside flowers. One is the sweet, watery liquid called *nectar*. The other is the yellow dustlike powder called *pollen*. A bee usually collects one of these substances at a time, although it can collect both on the same food-gathering trip.

The bee is guided to a flower by sharp eyes and two hornlike stalks on its head called *antennae*. A bee's antennae have a good sense of smell.

The bee collects nectar by poking its long, grooved tongue into a flower and sucking up the sweet, watery liquid at the flower's heart. This nectar flows from the bee's mouth into its crop, called a *honey bag*. Only a little nectar flows farther down into the bee's stomach, to be used as its own food. The rest remains in the crop, where liquid manufactured by the bee's body starts to turn the nectar into honey.

A bee collects pollen easily because pollen sticks to the fine hairs on the bee's body and legs. When those hairs are thickly covered, the bee packs the pollen for the trip home. First the bee's hairy front legs brush off the pollen on the front of its body and transfer it, along with the front legs' own load of pollen, to the middle pair of legs. Those legs transfer their load of pollen to the rear pair of legs. On each of the rear legs is a pocket that serves as a pollen carrying case. The bee's right rear leg brushes its pollen into the left leg's pocket. The left leg brushes its pollen into the right leg's pocket.

When a bee's honey bag is full of nectar, or when the pockets on its rear legs are packed with pollen, the bee flies back to its hive. Waiting for it are the thousands of worker honeybees whose jobs are carried out inside the hive. These *house bees*, as they are called, all depend on the food that the food-gathering bees bring home.

Each house bee has its own job. It may clean the hive or guard the hive's entrance. It may feed the queen, or feed the *larvae*, the sluglike forms that hatch out of the queen's eggs and that will become the next generation of bees. It may use the wax its body makes to help build the hundreds of tiny six-sided storage cells that fit together to form the hive's honeycombs. Or it may fill some of these cells with the nectar a food-gathering bee has brought in. Because bees live as they do, each playing its own part in their community, or society, they are called social insects.

To empty its honey bag, a returning food-gatherer forces some of the liquid in the bag up into its mouth. Then it transfers the nectar into the mouth of a house bee. The food-gatherer repeats this process until no nectar is left in the bag. A house bee that has received a mouthful of nectar first swallows a little of it, and then feeds some to other house bees by the same mouth-to-mouth method. Then it places any remaining nectar in an empty honeycomb cell.

In that cell the nectar is mixed with substances from house bees' bodies, and left to dry out until it becomes a heavy, sticky honey. Honey-filled cells are sealed with wax and kept sealed until winter comes. Then, when no fresh nectar can be found, the hive lives on the honey stored in its honeycombs.

To empty the pollen pockets on its rear legs, the returning food-gatherer uses its middle pair of legs to scrape the pollen

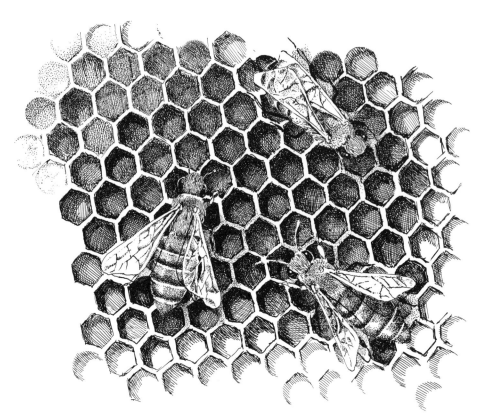

out and transfer it to honeycomb cells. House bees will mix the pollen with honey and feed it to the hive's larvae.

A food-gathering bee usually flies off again as soon as its pollen pockets and honey bag are empty. But if it has discovered a new feeding place—an orchard just beginning to bloom, perhaps—it may stay in the hive long enough to tell other bees how to get there.

The language the bee uses is a kind of dance. It may crawl in a circle, waggling its tail, or in a double circle like a figure 8. Its movements let the others know what direction to take and how far to fly to reach the new food source.

Bees have only one defense against enemies that want to steal their honey. They use their stingers. If a honey-seeking mouse enters a beehive, bees may sting it to death in minutes. But if honey-seeking ants invade the hive, the ants fight the defending bees by biting them. The battle may go on for hours, killing hundreds on both sides. Often the ants win.

A bee's stinger may also fail to protect the bee from enemies that catch bees because they want to eat them. Spiders spin webs that catch bees and hold them helpless before the bees have a chance to use their stingers. A toad waits beside a hive until a bee appears, and then flicks out its sticky tongue to pick up the bee. A praying mantis makes a quick meal out of the bee it seizes with its spiked forelegs. Swooping dragonflies catch bees and devour them.

Human beings, however, can be the bees' worst enemies. They destroy them with the poison sprays they use to kill harmful insects. The sprays stick to the pollen of flowers, and bees pick up the poison along with the pollen and carry it back to the hive. Larvae eat that poison-coated pollen, and it kills them.

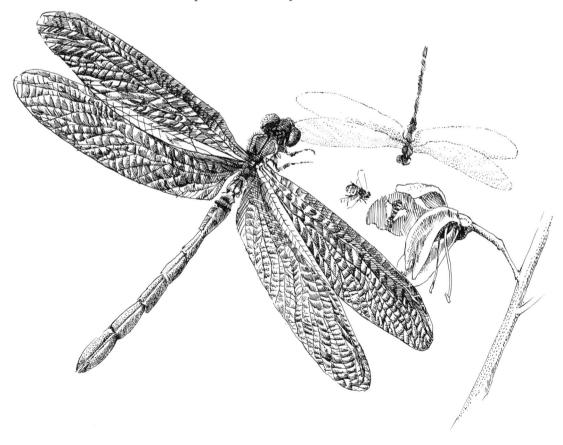

·MOSQUITOES·

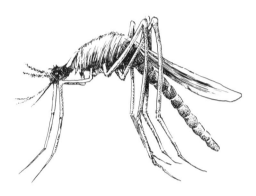

The insect we call a mosquito is really a delicate fly less than half an inch long. It has three pairs of thin legs, a pair of oval-shaped wings, and a pair of antennae in front of its eyes. Between the antennae is a tube called a *proboscis*. Through that tube the mosquito sucks up the flower nectar it lives on, just as an elephant sucks up water through its own proboscis, or trunk.

A female mosquito's proboscis is also used to get the extra food it needs to hatch its eggs. That food is the blood of a mammal—a human being, a dog, a horse, a cow, or some other warm-blooded animal. If you ever had a red, itchy spot on your arm—a spot you called a mosquito bite—that was the place where a female mosquito sucked up a tiny bit of your blood.

This is what happened: The mosquito's antennae led it to your arm. Her two feelers could sense your body by its warmth and moisture, and by the gas called *carbon dioxide*, which is part of the air you breathe out. The mosquito settled on your arm so lightly that you didn't feel it, although a moment before you might have heard the buzzing sound a female mosquito can make.

The mosquito gently tapped your skin with the tip of its proboscis. Then the outer covering of the proboscis slid up so that the two pairs of needlelike rods inside could go to work. The sawlike edges on the tips of one pair of rods fastened onto your skin. The sharp tips of the other pair pierced a hole there.

Into that hole in your skin the mosquito forced some of its saliva, which kept your blood from clotting, or getting thick. The saliva probably also caused the itching you soon felt at that place. Less than a minute after the mosquito landed on your arm, it was ready to suck up some of your blood. The sucking went on for only a few seconds—and then the mosquito flew off, ready to lay its eggs. Mosquitoes lay their eggs in water or in some other damp place. The water might be a pond, a puddle, a bird bath, or the rain water collected in an old tire or a plastic container that was tossed into a vacant lot.

Mosquito eggs quickly hatch into larvae, the second stage in this insect's life. Mosquito larvae look like tiny worms, with heads at one end and breathing tubes at the other. To get air as they feed on tiny bits of plant and animal life they find in their wet home, they often poke these tubes above the surface. The way the larvae move through the water has earned them the name *wrigglers*. A wriggler sheds its outer skin four times before it changes into the insect's next stage, called a *pupa*.

Mosquito pupae look like round heads attached to shrimplike tails that end in a pair of tiny paddles. Lashing those tails, the pupae, too, move through the water in a way that has earned

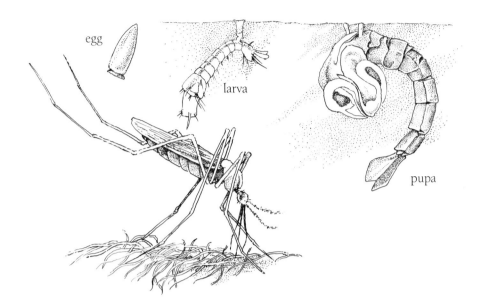

egg

larva

pupa

them a special name. They're called *tumblers*, and they have two short breathing tubes. A tumbler doesn't eat. After a few days, it changes and becomes a mosquito.

Mosquitoes have enemies at every stage of their lives. Fish eat their eggs, and the wrigglers and tumblers, too. So do dragonflies, which snatch them up from the water and swallow them. Dragonflies also gulp adult mosquitoes out of the air. A dragonfly can catch so many mosquitoes that it may have more than a hundred in its mouth at once. Spiders, lizards, and birds also like to eat mosquitoes.

Of course, human beings are enemies of mosquitoes because they know that some mosquitoes can carry diseases, and people just don't like female mosquitoes buzzing around and biting them. That's why people do their best to get rid of the damp and watery places where mosquitoes might lay their eggs. People also use sprays and other forms of insect control to destroy adult mosquitoes, mosquito eggs, wrigglers, and tumblers.

·PRAYING MANTISES·

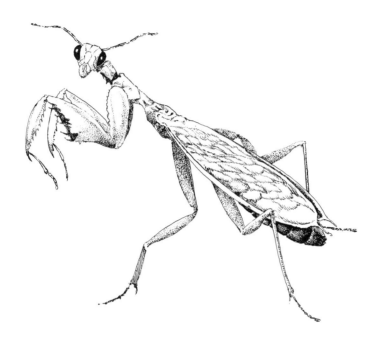

Every praying mantis is a thin sticklike insect with a pair of large eyes in its pointed head. But there are several different kinds of praying mantises. Some grow to be five inches long, and some are only half that big. Some are grayish green and others grayish brown. Some of the praying mantises that live in the tropics are as brilliantly colored as the flowers that grow there.

The praying mantis has two pairs of wings with which it can fly very well. And it has three pairs of legs. It walks on its middle and rear pairs of legs, which are long and thin. Its thicker front legs, covered with sharp spikes, are used for seizing and gripping the creatures it eats. The praying mantis was so named because it often sits perfectly still, holding its spiked legs together in front of its head, so that it looks as if it is praying.

A praying mantis eats almost any living creature it can catch. It chews and swallows bees, wasps, beetles, caterpillars, grasshoppers, crickets, butterflies, spiders, worms, small lizards and frogs, and young birds. Female praying mantises often eat their mates. Just-hatched baby praying mantises may even eat their baby brothers and sisters.

To get its food, a praying mantis usually sits still and waits silently for prey to come within reach. If it is a greenish mantis, it sits on something green—a leaf, a twig, a flower stalk. If it is a brownish mantis, it sits on something brown. Against this matching background the mantis becomes almost invisible, and

you might stare straight at a praying mantis only a foot away and not notice it. The creatures it likes to eat may also get close to a praying mantis without noticing it. While a praying mantis waits for one of them to appear, its head swings slowly around and up and down so that it can see anything that approaches. The praying mantis is the only insect that can move its head the way you can, without moving its body.

Let's say a caterpillar is crawling across a leaf, inching closer and closer to the praying mantis that is watching it. Suddenly, in the blink of an eye—in one-twentieth of a second—powerful forelegs dart out and grab the caterpillar. The caterpillar is still struggling inside that trap as the jaws of the praying mantis close on it. Biting off one piece after another, the praying mantis chews and swallows without stopping until the caterpillar has been completely eaten.

Or let's say a praying mantis sees a cricket far out of its reach. Then the mantis may move toward the cricket so slowly and carefully that the cricket doesn't even try to escape until it's too late.

In the fall, a female praying mantis lays her eggs in an egg case about the size of a walnut, which is attached to a twig or a plant stem. The case is formed out of the sticky white foam the female mantis can produce from the tip of her tail. As soon as the eggs are laid and sealed in that case, the praying mantis simply walks away to continue her steady search for food.

The surface of the egg case turns brown and hardens. Unless mice gnaw at it or woodpeckers attack it, the eggs are safe inside the case until spring. Then tiny baby praying mantises emerge from the egg case and begin their own search for food.

At first these babies eat only very small insects, such as *aphids*, and their own bodies are so soft that ants like to eat them. But their bodies harden and grow quickly, and soon their powerful forelegs are capturing any prey unwary enough to get close to them.

Fierce as a praying mantis is, it does have enemies. A snake or an insect-eating bird will eat adult praying mantises whenever possible. Sometimes a praying mantis can save itself by using its forelegs to "box" with a small bird or snake. Sometimes it can fly to safety. Most of the time, however, the praying mantis's enemies leave it alone because they simply don't see it against its protective brown or green background.

·MONARCH BUTTERFLIES·

The best-known butterfly in North America is probably the monarch, which measures about four inches from the tip of one opened wing to the tip of the other. Those handsome wings are a brilliant orange, edged with black bands dotted with yellow and white spots. Like all butterflies, the monarch has six legs, four wings, a pair of antennae, and two eyes. It also has a proboscis coiled up beneath its head, through which it sucks up the flower nectar that is its only food.

With a magnifying glass, you could see what happens when a monarch lands on a flower. Through the glass you could watch the monarch's proboscis uncoil, stretch deep into the heart of the flower, and suck up the sweet liquid. When no nectar is left, the tube coils back up again, and the monarch flies off to find another flower that will provide it with food.

Monarchs are sometimes called *milkweed butterflies* because female monarchs always lay their eggs on the underside of a leaf of the milkweed plant—usually one egg to a leaf. These eggs hatch into caterpillarlike larvae that begin to eat immediately.

A larva first eats up what is left of its own egg. Next it chews up the tender parts of the leaf on which the egg was laid. And from then on it crawls from one leaf to another, eating as it goes.

Soon the larva has eaten so much that its skin bursts open. The larva wriggles out, wearing a new skin loose enough to give it room to go on growing. This process is called *molting*. A monarch larva eats so much, and eats so fast, that it molts four times during the two weeks after its birth.

At the end of that time the larva is about two inches long, and its last skin is striped in yellow, black, and white. The larva has now finished eating and is ready to change its form. As it hangs head down from a leaf or a twig, its skin splits open once more and falls away, leaving a green shell behind. Inside that shell is a pupa, or *chrysalis*, the next stage in the butterfly's life. A pupa needs no food at all.

After about ten days, a full-grown butterfly emerges from the shell. It rests until its wet, crumpled wings dry out and stiffen, and then it takes off into the air.

Three generations of monarchs may be born and die during a summer. But when autumn arrives, thousands of those born late in the season set off on a remarkable journey. Leaving their birthplaces in Canada and the northern United States, they

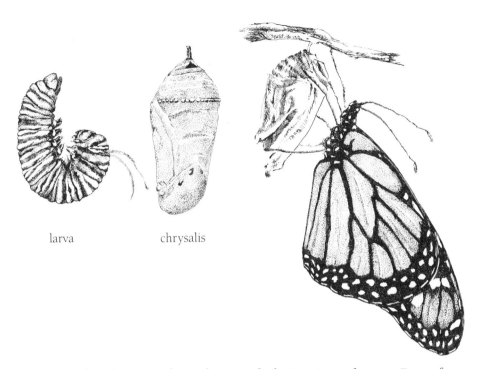

larva   chrysalis

migrate, heading southward toward their winter home. Day after day they fly steadily on, against winds that can leave their wings ragged and tattered. Each night they rest in the same trees migrating monarchs rested in the year before. Each morning they take off again. Finally they settle where monarchs have spent many winters, in Florida, Louisiana, southern Texas, Mexico, and the Caribbean Islands.

Milkweed plants grow in all those places. And before the female monarchs die, those exhausted travelers lay eggs under the leaves of the milkweed plants. In the spring the new young butterflies, nourished on milkweed, start migrating north. After laying eggs of their own under milkweed leaves, some females die on the way. Their eggs develop into butterflies that join the long parade that for weeks flies across the sky.

No one knows how the monarchs of one generation can find their way to the winter home of their ancestors—a home they have never seen. No one knows how later generations can fly back to the very places their parents or grandparents migrated from the year before. But we do know that monarchs survive only because they can find the special food they need at both ends of their astonishing migrations.

The monarch butterfly's diet of milkweed plants keeps it unusually safe from insect-eating birds. The diet gives monarch larvae, and adult monarchs, too, such a bitter taste that birds vomit after eating a single one of them. So birds generally avoid all orange-and-black-and-white-and-yellow butterflies. A monarch's most dangerous enemy is probably the praying mantis, which eats almost anything, no matter how it tastes.

·ANTS·

Ants may be black or brownish or red. There are more than two thousand kinds, some only an eighth of an inch long, others a full half-inch in length. But all ants are alike in some ways. Their bodies, protected by a shell-like covering, have three parts: a head at one end, an abdomen at the other, and a part in-between called the *thorax*. And all ants have two eyes, a pair of antennae, and powerful jaws for digging and chewing.

Ants, like bees, are social insects, and all the ants in a colony, or family, work together for the colony's benefit. Some worker ants never leave their underground nest. They feed and take care of their queens, the hundreds of eggs the queens lay, and the tiny larvae that hatch from those eggs. They keep the nest clean, protect it from enemies, and store food for the winter, when no fresh food can be brought in. Other worker ants must leave the nest to find and bring home all the food the colony needs. These are the ants you see scurrying about aboveground.

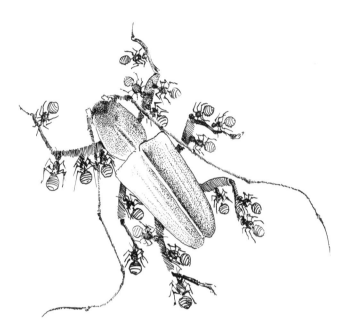

Different ants eat different foods. Some eat dead insects and spiders. Others eat flower nectar or the sticky liquids that ooze from tree buds and the tiny bodies of aphids. Some eat seeds. Some eat all of these.

Let's say you were watching a small brown ant come out of its nest and move quickly away from it. With patience and a magnifying glass, you could see how it goes about its job of finding food.

Its eyes, one on each side of its head, can see very little. But its long antennae serve as its nose and have a good sense of touch. By waving its antennae about and using them to tap the ground, the ant feels and smells its way along. To keep the antennae clean, the ant often stops to draw them through its *combs*, the rows of hairs on its front legs.

Suddenly the ant stops. Its antennae have sent a signal that says, "This feels good and smells good." The ant rasps its ridged lip across the object in front of it, scraping off tiny bits.

Through your magnifying glass, you might be able to learn that the ant has found part of a dead fly and has grasped bits of it in its jaws. But even with a magnifying glass, you couldn't learn what happens to those bits.

First the ant's strong jaws grind the bits of fly into a paste. Then, by mixing that paste with its own mouth juices, the ant turns part of the paste into a liquid that it can swallow. The rest of the paste moves into a pocketlike space below the ant's mouth, where the paste is squeezed until it yields more liquid. The ant swallows that, too, and spits out the small pill of dry stuff left in the pocket.

The swallowed liquid goes down into the ant's crop, sometimes called its *social stomach*. Most of the liquid remains there to be shared later with other ants in the nest. A small amount of the liquid goes from the crop to a second, lower stomach, for the ant itself to use as food.

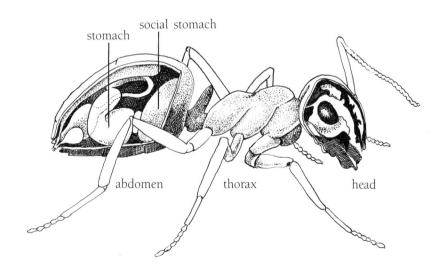

When the last bit of fly has been eaten, the ant continues its search for food. If it finds a seed, the seed must also be ground to a paste and mixed with liquid before it can be swallowed. But flower nectar and other liquids can be swallowed immediately.

When its social stomach is full, the food-gathering ant returns to the nest to share its stomach contents with the ants that work there. This is how ants share food: The food-carrying ant meets a hungry ant, and their antennae touch. Ants almost always touch antennae when they meet, but this particular touching probably signals that the hungry ant wants food. Then both ants rise on their back legs. They stand face to face, with their antennae still touching. Their mouths meet. The food-bearing ant brings some of the liquid in its crop up into its mouth, and lets that liquid flow into the mouth of the hungry ant.

By the same mouth-to-mouth method, the ant that has been fed will feed some of that liquid to others in the colony. If its job is to take care of the queen, it gives her some. If it is a larvae nurse, it puts some of the liquid into the larvae's mouths. At the same time, the larvae nurse gets extra food for itself by licking up the moisture oozing from the larvae's bodies.

Food-gathering ants may also pick up in their jaws, and bring back to the nest, bits of undigested dead insects, seeds, and other foods. These are stored in the nest until they are needed. Then, perhaps in winter, members of the colony grind these foods into a paste and transform them into the liquid form the ants are able to swallow.

Ants can live as long as six years. But any ant outside its nest is always in danger of being eaten by one of its many enemies. Larger ants and other insects are among those enemies. So are spiders, frogs, toads, lizards, praying mantises, woodpeckers, and other birds. Or an ant may be killed by a human being who thinks all ants are a nuisance.

·SPIDERS·

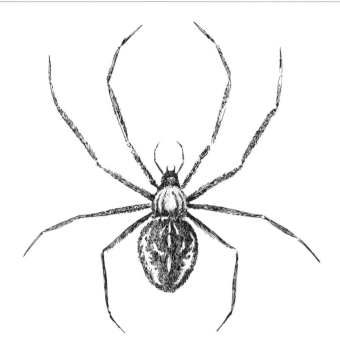

Just as there are thousands of different ants, there are thousands of different spiders. Some spiders are only a quarter of an inch across. Some are large enough to spread out over a saucer. Some are a dull black or brown; others are brightly colored or striped.

The body of a spider has two parts, one much larger than the other. These are connected by a narrow waist. A spider's eight legs, each with seven joints and ending in tiny claws, are attached to the front and smaller part of its body. Most spiders have eight eyes, although some have fewer—six or four or only two. Just behind a spider's eyes is a pair of jointed feelers called *pedipalps*. Spiders' bodies are well equipped to capture and kill the many different kinds of insects they live on, such as flies, wasps, beetles, mosquitoes, butterflies, moths, grasshoppers, and crickets. A spider's jaws have sharp fangs that can seize and hold its prey.

One way spiders capture their live food is by weaving a trap in the form of a web. The web is woven out of silklike thread that is produced when a spider forces a special liquid out of tubes at the back of its body. This liquid hardens into thread as soon as it is exposed to the air. The spider's body also manufactures a gluelike substance that forms tiny sticky drops along those threads. The drops hold any insect that touches them.

A spiderweb may look like a wheel, with spokes and a central hub surrounded by larger and larger circles. The wheel hangs in the air like a curtain, fastened at its edges to tree branches or other supports. Because it is almost invisible, insects fly into the web. You might walk into it yourself, and feel the sticky threads clinging to your face.

Another kind of web is stretched out horizontally, to catch insects that fall into it from above.

A third kind of web is shaped like a funnel. There is a platform at the funnel's wide, open end, and insects fall or stumble onto it.

Or a spiderweb may be just a tangle of threads near the ground. It might look as if its maker knew nothing at all about web-weaving, but this tangle is as efficient as any other web at holding insects that walk or crawl or tumble into it.

A spider may stay at the center of its web or wait hidden at the edge of it. Some spiders stay out of sight in underground tunnels, attached by threads to the webs they have built aboveground nearby.

A spider knows instantly when an insect has been trapped in

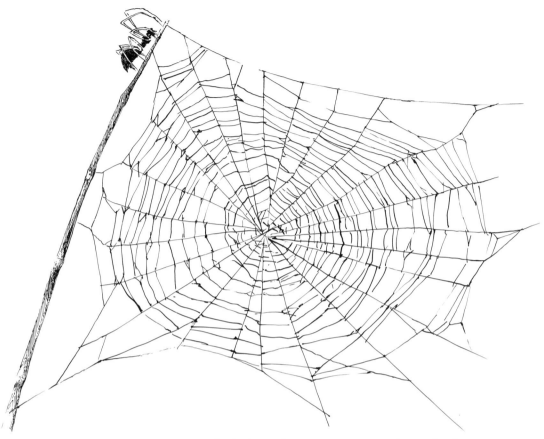

its web. Its sensitive legs feel the vibrations set up through the threads as the trapped insect struggles to escape. Then the spider rushes out to see what it has caught.

But not all spiders depend on webs for catching their food. Some hunt insects instead, or lie in wait for them and sieze them before they can escape.

The *spitting spider*, for example, uses its front legs to feel for hidden insects. When it finds one, it spits out a sticky glue that pins down the insect. The spider can then eat it at leisure.

The powerful-legged *wolf spider* has much better eyes than most spiders have. It can see an insect at a distance, and then run it down.

A *jumping spider* creeps toward its prey until, suddenly, it leaps into the air and lands on the insect. A human being who could jump as well as this spider would be able to jump about forty feet.

A spider may hide in a crack in tree bark and reach out to snap up an unwary beetle passing by. A yellow spider may wait on a yellow flower and catch a butterfly that lands beside it without noticing its presence.

Like the food of ants, a spider's food must be liquid. So when a spider's fangs close on a small insect, they first inject the insect with a poison that paralyzes it. Then the fangs inject the insect with another substance that turns the soft parts of the insect's body into a liquid that the spider can suck up.

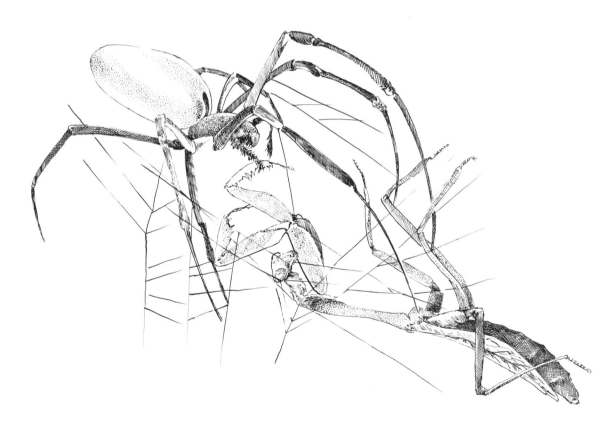

Sometimes a web traps an insect or butterfly that the spider doesn't like and doesn't want to eat. Then the spider may get rid of its captive by cutting away the part of the web that holds it. Also, if a spider catches and paralyzes a victim that it doesn't want to eat immediately, it can wrap the insect up neatly with the same threads it uses to make a web and carry it away.

Spiders never carry such food to their young. Spider mothers do spin cocoons around the eggs they lay, which usually keep the eggs safe. But the tiny baby spiders that hatch from the eggs have to feed themselves. So the babies of web-weaving spiders, for example, must try to catch insects by weaving miniature webs like those their mothers make.

Frogs, toads, lizards, and many birds catch and eat spiders. One of their enemies is a wasp that catches spiders and paralyzes them by stinging them—just as spiders paralyze their own victims. Then the wasp stuffs the helpless spider into a tunnel it has dug in the ground. When the tunnel is full of still-living but paralyzed spiders, the wasp lays an egg on top of them and seals the tunnel shut. The larva that hatches out of that egg will thus have plenty of live food to eat while it is developing into a wasp.

Another deadly enemy of the spider is a fly that lays its eggs under the skin of a spider's back. The larva that hatches out of that egg lives on the juices of its helpless host until the spider dies, and then the larva eats the spider's dead body.

Spiders even have enemies of their own kind—cannibal spiders, which eat other spiders.

·LADYBUGS AND FIREFLIES·

People sometimes say they don't like the insects called *beetles*. But when they think about it, they usually realize there are two beetles they do like. One is the little insect named in the nursery rhyme that begins, "Ladybug, ladybug, fly away home."

Sometimes called a *ladybird*, a ladybug looks like half of a tiny round ball, colored yellow or orange-red, with black spots. What seems to be its hard shell is really its front pair of wings, which meet over its back and cover its body. The ladybug's six short legs, head, and two antennae poke out from under them. When a ladybug is about to fly, the front wings separate and open out. Then its rear pair of wings, beneath them, can spread wide and carry the ladybug through the air.

A ladybug has a powerful pair of jaws, with which it seizes and chews up the insects it lives on. Some of the insects it likes best are those most harmful to plants and trees—aphids, for example, and the tiny insects called *scales*. That's why ladybugs are always welcome on a farm or in a garden.

A ladybug lays small batches of its yellow eggs on plants or trees infested by aphids or some other harmful insects. In this way it provides food for the larvae that will hatch from those eggs. The larvae are wormlike creatures that can get about rapidly on their long legs. They have very large appetites and begin immediately to close their jaws on mouthful after mouthful of insects.

But a ladybug larva can't eat solid food. So the larva injects some of its saliva into the insects to turn them into a liquid.

Ladybugs and their larvae have many enemies. Birds may eat them. Wasps sting them and put them into their nests so their own larvae can eat them.

When ladybugs and their larvae are eating aphids, they are especially threatened by ants. Ants want aphids kept alive, because ants are very fond of the honeylike substance that oozes from aphids' bodies. But a ladybug can squeeze from its leg joints a bit of blood that tastes and smells so bad that ants often back away from it, just as birds do. And a ladybug larva tastes so unpleasant to an ant that, after eating one of them, an ant may try to chase the next one away instead of snapping it up.

Fireflies, sometimes called *lightning bugs*, are the other kind of beetle that many people agree they like. A firefly isn't brightly colored, so you might not notice it even if it was very close to you. Its body, usually about half an inch long, is a dull brown or black. Even the red, orange, or yellow patches on its wings are so dull you would have to look closely to see them. But on summer nights fireflies light up with such a bright glow that people say, "Look! The fireflies are out!"

A firefly can flash its light—caused by chemicals in the lower rear part of its body—on and off in a sort of code, or signal. Each of the many kinds of fireflies has its own code, and fireflies use these codes to find their mates. A male flashes its own special signal, which can be seen by females hidden close to the ground. If a female answers with the same kind of signal, the two fireflies mate. The female then lays her eggs in moist soil, often under rotting wood or rubbish heaps.

Adult fireflies may eat nectar and pollen, or may eat nothing at all. But the rather flat brown larvae that hatch out of their eggs have large appetites, and jaws good for grasping and holding the small insects, worms, and snails they find on the ground.

But, like the larvae of ladybugs, firefly larvae can't eat solid food. So they, too, must use injections of saliva to turn their prey into liquid.

If firefly larvae don't stay well hidden, they will become food themselves for birds, frogs, or toads. Those same enemies eat adult fireflies, too. Frogs have been known to eat so many that they glow from the light of the fireflies in their stomachs.

Male fireflies have another enemy, a certain kind of female firefly that watches for the flashing signals of males that aren't the same kind of firefly she is. When she sees one of those signals, she flashes an answer in the same code. Then the male, mistaking her for a firefly of its own kind, flies to meet her—and she eats him.

·EARTHWORMS·

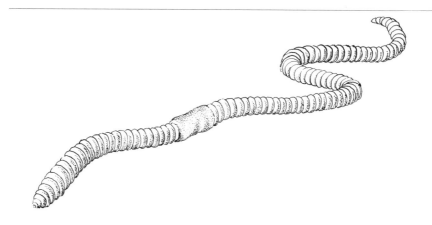

An earthworm's body, inside its soft skin, is made up of rings, called *segments*, held together by muscles. Earthworms may have from fifty to several hundred segments. It's hard to tell how long a particular earthworm really is, because one set of its muscles can stretch it out or shorten it. An earthworm can therefore be three inches long at one moment and five inches long a moment later.

An earthworm doesn't have a real head and doesn't have eyes. But it has a mouth at one end of its body and a kind of tail at the other. Short stiff hairs on each of its segments act like the spikes on a runner's track shoes. They give the earthworm a good grip, even on slippery soil, as it moves about in search of the tiny bits of plants and dead insects it lives on.

Unless you know where and when to look, seeing an earthworm isn't easy. The reason for this is that the earthworm breathes through its skin and can breathe only when its skin is moist and cool. Because an earthworm must stay where hot sunlight can't reach it, it spends most of its life in the tunnel it digs for itself. The length of the tunnel may be as short as a few inches or as long as several feet. Each earthworm digs down as far as it has to go to reach a place where it is safe from heat and dryness.

You might wonder how a soft earthworm can dig even a short tunnel through hard earth, and how it can get enough to eat if it spends so much of its life underground. The earthworm has solved both of those problems very well.

To start digging its tunnel, the earthworm bites up a mouthful of earth and swallows it. Then it takes another mouthful and another. Head first, bite by bite, it chews its way downward. And in each bite it swallows, there are at least a few of the tiny bits of food it needs.

But the earthworm must get rid of the parts of each mouthful that it can't digest—sand, for example, and grit. To do that it crawls back to the surface from time to time. There, through an opening in its tail, it pushes that material out of its body in the form of pinhead-size balls, called *castings*. A little pile of castings, perhaps half-hidden in the grass, tells you that there is an earthworm's tunnel at that spot.

Earthworms' tunnels and castings both make soil better for growing plants. The tunnels do this by letting air and moisture deep into the soil. The castings do it by bringing a fresh layer of soil to the surface. That's why gardeners and farmers are happy to have large populations of earthworms in their land.

The openings to many earthworm tunnels are hidden beneath some covering, such as a rock or a piece of bark. Even in daytime, an earthworm can safely come out of such a tunnel and crawl around under that rooflike protection looking for food. But if its tunnel opening is not protected, an earthworm comes out only after dark, during cloudy or rainy days when the sun can't harm it, or when its tunnel is flooded by heavy rains. Even then the earthworm usually keeps its tail inside the tunnel, so that if danger threatens it can back down quickly into safety.

An earthworm doesn't have to feed its babies. When it is ready to lay its eggs, it makes a cocoon out of substances from its body to hold the eggs and some food its body also produces. And when the tiny baby earthworms hatch from the eggs and emerge from the cocoon, they are able to take care of themselves.

Earthworms have many enemies. Some snakes eat them. So do toads and birds, particularly robins. Even deep inside their tunnels, earthworms are not always safe. Skunks dig into the ground to find and eat them. Moles, digging their own tunnels, eat any earthworms they find. But these small creatures, which look so helpless and face so many dangers, may live for ten years or even longer.

Do you think now that someday, when you're very hungry, you might nibble on an insect or two? You probably wouldn't, and that would be wise, because human beings would have trouble digesting most of the foods that form the regular diet of squirrels, birds, and the other creatures in this book.

But haven't all these creatures worked out remarkably successful ways of getting the food they need without leaving their homes in parks or gardens or vacant lots—without ever having to go to a store?

·Index·

EDUCATION